WRITE LIKE A PRO™

WRITING PERSONAL STORIES

JAYE E. COOK and LAUREN SPENCER

rosen publishing's
rosen central®

New York

Published in 2012 by The Rosen Publishing Group, Inc.
29 East 21st Street, New York, NY 10010

First Edition

Library of Congress Cataloging-in-Publication Data

Cook, Jaye E.
Writing personal stories/Jaye E. Cook, Lauren Spencer.—1st ed.
     p. cm.—(Write like a pro)
Includes bibliographical references and index.
ISBN 978-1-4488-4684-9 (library binding)
ISBN 978-1-4488-4690-0 (pbk.)
ISBN 978-1 4488-4748-8 (6-pack)
1. Autobiography—Authorship—Juvenile literature. I. Spencer, Lauren. II. Title.
CT25.C685 2012
808'.06692—dc22

                                                                    2010050039

Manufactured in the United States of America

CPSIA Compliance Information: Batch #S11YA: For further information, contact Rosen Publishing, New York, New York, at
1-800-237-9932.

CONTENTS

INTRODUCTION

Personal writing is a great way for an author to communicate how he or she feels about the world. Authors can find many ways to express themselves by writing their personal stories, either in their own private journals or in a form to share with others. Whether the work is kept private or not, personal writing offers a distinct view into the mind of the author.

There are many different forms of personal writing. A piece can take the form of a narrative, which uses traditional storytelling techniques like setting, plot, and dialogue. Poetry and free verse are more freestyle forms of expression. Letters and e-mails are also fun forms in which to write about and share personal experiences. Journal writing is an expression of the author's innermost thoughts, often recorded with privacy in mind. On the other hand, a blog is an online journal that the public can read. Although it is not as personal as a private journal, a blog also reflects the personality of the author. Whatever form of personal writing you choose, your goal is to find pleasure in your expression.

Personal writing depends on the author's observations and thoughts. It usually does not rely heavily on facts or research. Personal writing can serve all kinds of functions, from remembering and recording memories, to communicating feelings and emotions, to sharing an event with a friend. Today, in the age of the Internet, there are more ways than ever to create and share your personal stories.

This book will examine the various stages in which personal writing takes shape—choosing a topic and style, writing drafts, and then polishing and presenting your work. Ultimately, your goal is to encourage the writer inside of you while enjoying the journey of creative expression.

chapter 1

Forms of Personal Writing

All personal writing comes from an author's own life and connects to his or her own experiences. Various forms and styles can be used when writing from a personal perspective.

Each of the forms discussed in this chapter serves a specific purpose. Personal narratives tell a story. Personal letters or e-mails share accounts of events or thoughts with someone else. Poems express experiences through vivid descriptive language, sound, and rhythm. Journals reflect the author's thoughts and feelings and may be shared with others or kept private. Blogs are online journals that are usually shared.

The different forms of personal writing can lend themselves to any story. Before starting a first draft of a personal story, pinpoint what form you'll be

ESSENTIAL STEPS

Explore the different forms of personal writing.

Try various forms and styles to help you find your author's voice.

using for your piece. If the first one doesn't suit your story, try another.

Personal Narrative

The personal narrative is the retelling of an event in someone's life. It has a specific format that includes a beginning, middle, and end. A personal narrative often uses familiar story elements such as setting, characters, and plot. The plot is the series of actions that make up your story.

A personal narrative often details an event or series of events in the order in which they happened. This is also known as chronological order. A good narrative brings the unique details of an event to life. The excerpt on page 9 is the beginning of a narrative about an airplane trip to Puerto Rico.

Sometimes the word "memoir" is used to

Best-selling author Maya Angelou signs a reader's copy of her latest book. She is known for writing vivid and poetic descriptions of her life experiences and relationships.

Document1

"We're late!" I heard my mother screech. She shook my brother Eddie and me awake. "Throw on something, anything! We've got to get to the airport!"

On this chilly December day, we had tickets to fly to Puerto Rico to visit my Uncle Hector for the holidays. We had been looking forward to this trip for a long time. My mom had stayed up late to finish packing suitcases and wrapping presents. Now, she looked like a wreck, with a messy ponytail on top of her head and dark circles under her eyes. She must have slept right through her alarm.

Within a few minutes, Eddie and I piled into the back seat of the Chevy next to our baby sister, Rosie, who was cooing happily in her car seat. My mother was less content.

"Traffic—that's just great!" she grumbled as we joined the other cars on the highway.

Page 1   Sec 1   1/1   0/0   ○REC ○TRK ○EXT ○OVR

describe this type of writing. A memoir is an autobiographical piece that spans different moments in the author's life, rather than highlighting only one specific moment.

It is important to note that a memoir is a form of nonfiction. Someone who reads a memoir expects the events described in it to be true—to actually have occurred in the author's real life. Some writers have landed in hot water for publishing "fiction-enhanced" memoirs. These authors added fictional events to their life stories to make them more entertaining, but did not let their readers know. It is acceptable to create a work about oneself that includes made-up events. However, a responsible author presents such work as fiction, not memoir.

Personal Letters and E-mails

Writing a letter to a friend or relative is a fun, expressive way to share an experience. A personal letter is usually written using an upbeat, friendly tone. When writing a letter, you can imagine that your reader is listening to your story. Be as detailed as you can in describing your topic. Personal questions aimed at the person receiving the letter are a thoughtful way to connect to your reader. You can also use rhetorical questions, which are questions asked for effect with no expected answers. If you like, include a joke, poem, or sketch that your reader might enjoy.

There are several formatting requirements to follow when writing a friendly letter. The heading appears at the top of the letter. It includes your address and the date aligned to the right-hand margin. Below the heading, a salutation greets the person to whom you're writing, using "Dear so-and-so." A very casual letter or e-mail can have a more informal greeting. Write the salutation aligned to the left-hand margin, and use a comma after the person's name.

The body of the letter includes your thoughts and ideas. Use short paragraphs to hold the reader's attention. Indent to mark the beginning of each new paragraph. If you are skipping lines between paragraphs, do not indent.

Document1

111 Everywhere Street
Littletown, CT 33399
January 6, 2011

Dear Samantha,

I just returned from Puerto Rico, where I was visiting my uncle for the holidays. It was difficult getting there. First, my mom overslept and we almost missed our flight. Then, the airplane ride was a nightmare. It made me remember the first time I was on a plane. I was six years old at the time, and I clutched my mother's hands for dear life! This time, the problem was that a huge storm was approaching.

Right after we took off, the plane started bouncing. At one point, I made a loud noise, and a passenger stared at me with an angry look. I felt sort of silly, but what was her problem? I mean, hadn't she ever seen anyone startled before? Actually, I think she was just as afraid as I was.

Although it seemed like forever, we finally did touch down in Puerto Rico. We had a wonderful time there. How was your holiday? Write me back and let me know!

Your friend,
Miguel

Page 1   Sec 1   1/1   At 1"   ○REC ○TRK ○EXT ○OVR

Two lines below the last sentence, say good-bye to your friend with a closing on one line and your signature below it. The closing uses a phrase such as "Sincerely," "Your friend," or "Love," followed by a comma.

Writing a personal e-mail is similar to writing a letter, except that it is more casual and it arrives in the recipient's inbox immediately. When sending

---

New Message

Send Chat Attach Address Fonts Colors Save As Draft   Photo Browser Show Stationery

To: Matt@emailaddress.com

Cc:

Bcc:

Subject: Happy New Year!

Hi Matt,

Happy New Year! How was your winter break? We had a lot of fun visiting my Uncle Hector in Puerto Rico. The island was beautiful, and we ate a lot of delicious food.

Our trip had a rough start. We overslept and almost missed our flight. We were running through the airport when the airport employee driving the courtesy cart told us to hop on. He rushed us to our gate and we made the flight!

Look forward to seeing you at school and hearing about your vacation.

Miguel

an e-mail, you need to enter a title in the subject line and your friend's e-mail address after "To." Your e-mail address and the date of your message will appear automatically in your friend's inbox.

Personal Journals

Journal or diary writing is a form of personal composition that is often kept private. A journal can be a great resource for any writer. Keeping a journal can help a writer clarify ideas and feelings so that a situation can be better understood. Writing in a journal is good practice for putting pen to paper on a daily basis and can help you become a better writer.

Establish a regular time to write in your journal each day or evening, and it will become a habit. Make sure the time and place where you choose to write are convenient and quiet, if necessary. (While some people can write while it's noisy, others need complete silence in order to concentrate.)

When keeping a journal, begin by writing for a set length of time each day. Five to ten minutes is a good start. After a few weeks, increase your writing time to fifteen to twenty minutes. After a while, your writing will improve, as will your fluency as a writer. You can also experiment with different forms and styles

December 18, 2010

Today, we flew to Puerto Rico to see Uncle Hector. The flight was scary, but I learned that I can get through anything as long as I remain calm. I think mom was as frightened as I was about the bumpy flight. Although she was pretending to be asleep, I saw her foot wiggling rapidly like she was nervous. At one point, I felt angry because a woman started staring at me.

Anyway, when we landed, Uncle Hector was waiting. Puerto Rico is beautiful, and the ocean is right outside of his house. I'll have to investigate the surroundings tomorrow; now I'm exhausted.

in your journal, such as poetry or short stories. Remember to date each entry.

Poetry

Poetry is a unique form of personal writing. Poetry looks different from prose because it is not written in sentences and paragraphs. Instead,

TRADITIONAL FORMS OF POETRY

Ballad A poem that tells a story, such as "All the World's a Stage" by sixteenth-century English poet William Shakespeare.

Blank verse Unrhymed poetry with meter.

Elegy A sad poem, such as "A Refusal to Mourn the Death, by Fire, of a Child in London" by the twentieth-century English poet Dylan Thomas.

Epic A long story poem that usually tells about the adventures of a hero, such as *The Odyssey* by the ancient Greek poet Homer.

Free verse Poetry that does not follow a specific meter or rhyme scheme.

Haiku A form of Japanese poetry that is three lines in length, each line with a specific number of syllables.

Lyric A short poem that expresses personal emotions.

Ode A long poem that is rich in poetic devices and imagery, such as "Ode to the West Wind" by eighteenth-century English poet Percy Bysshe Shelley.

Sonnet A fourteen-line poem, such as "Shall I Compare Thee to a Summer's Day" by Shakespeare.

it is written in lines and stanzas, or groups of lines. Poetry depends on rich descriptions to bring a situation to life. A poem comes primarily from the author's senses and innermost feelings.

Many different styles of poetry exist. Many traditional poems have a regular beat and a set length to each line. They often, though not always, have lines that rhyme. For example, a haiku is a traditional Japanese poem that is three lines in length. The first line contains five syllables; the second, seven; and the third, five. Although the haiku was once reserved for expressing themes about nature, this form is now used to express almost anything. Example:

Air Power

What a rush I feel,
When the airplane soars madly.
Over clouds it dips.

Miguel Ferrer

While many traditional forms are still used today, most contemporary poetry is written in free verse, meaning that there is no set rhythm or rhyme. In a free-verse poem, the poet expresses related thoughts, allowing the lines to end where they feel natural and effective. Free-verse poetry does not require any set meter (a measured rhythm), length, or rhyme scheme. Example:

Aerophobia

Sky so blue
floating above the clouds.
White, rough,
the plane bumps.
Suddenly,
a pair of eyes behind glasses
look at me hard and hold me in their sight.
I realize I must have let out a scream
as the bump bounced me
into the land of the scared.

Miguel Ferrer

Poetry allows authors to play with the sounds of words. For that reason, poetry is usually most effective when it is read aloud. Here are a few techniques to make your poetry sing:

• Repetition of the same words, such

A SECOND LOOK

Could my piece be written in various ways?

Which style best reflects my personal experience?

as "I can," at the beginning of each line gives a poem rhythm.

- Using multiple words that start with the same sound is called alliteration. "Sparkling stars smile above the solitary sea."
- Using words that contain the same vowel sounds is called assonance. "At daybreak, a flag waved in the stadium."

Onomatopoeia is the use of words to imitate the sounds they describe. "Bing-bong, the seatbelt signs came on."

For a full range of poetry forms and styles, look at poetry Web sites, such as http://www.poets.org from the Academy of American Poets, or look at books about poetry in a library.

There are as many methods for creating expressive pieces of personal writing as there are ideas. Try different techniques depending on your topic and your audience. If the first one fails to interest you, try another.

Allow yourself to explore your author's voice. This is the inner voice inside of you that is yours alone. Your author's voice is what will allow you to express yourself as a creative individual.

chapter 2

Getting Started: Prewriting

Authors use a multistep process to take a memory or an observation and grow it into a great piece of personal writing. Whether you are writing on your own or are completing an assignment for school, learning the stages of the writing process—and some of the special techniques of the writer's craft—will help you succeed in your personal writing.

At the start of a writing project, known as the prewriting stage, a writer explores possible topics before selecting one. Also, the writer gathers details and facts that will make the piece more interesting. How well a personal story works often depends on the richness of its descriptions. Concentrating on the five senses can help personal writing reach a height of expression. This chapter discusses a number of methods you can use to gather and pin down your story's rich details before writing a first draft.

Finding a Topic

ESSENTIAL STEPS

Survey the variety of ideas and topics that are available to you.

Choose a topic.

Find and create details to support your chosen topic.

The best way to write an effective piece of personal writing is to choose a topic you feel strongly about. Although many subjects would make great writing topics, decide on one idea to explore.

Since personal writing depends on your connection to the subject, choose a topic that allows you to express yourself fully. Good topics often revolve around things you have enjoyed, such as an event in your own life. Focus on a moment in which every one of your senses was alive. This can range from a memory of a birthday party or celebration, to your first meeting with someone, to an especially scary experience such as spending a night in a strange place. Pull out a blank piece of paper and begin the process of brainstorming, or freely jotting down your initial ideas.

One way to get your thoughts flowing is to organize your ideas in a sensory details chart. Along the side of the page, write out the five senses (sight, smell, hearing, touch, taste). Think about the experience that you intend to describe in your story. Then, list any

SENSORY DETAILS CHART

EVENT **AN AFTERNOON AT THE BEACH**

VISUAL DETAILS
- sun sparkling on the water
- colorful umbrellas dotting the sand
- people of all ages swimming in the ocean

SOUNDS
- children yelling and laughing
- seagulls squawking
- waves crashing on the shore

SMELLS
- coconut-scented suntan lotion
- salty smell of sea spray
- hot dogs roasting

TASTES
- ice cream bar melting on my tongue
- cold iced tea

FEELINGS/ TEXTURES
- hot, dry sand
- sun baking my skin
- cold splash of the waves on my feet
- ocean breeze blowing my hair

moments when you experienced those senses in an extreme way. Include as many details as you can. You will probably come across at least one moment on your list that really satisfies all of the senses and would therefore make an exciting focus for your piece.

Collecting Details

Once you've decided on your topic, you can focus on the other elements surrounding the experience. At this stage, you should gather all of the raw material for your writing.

Although personal writing requires little research beyond examining items that may jog your memory, begin with some facts to help you create an interesting piece. Think about people who can answer questions about the moment you are exploring, such as someone else who was there or a person whom you told about the event. Examining photos or mementos might be helpful if the event occurred a long time ago.

A great way to get your topic organized is to use a "Five W's" chart to outline the event. Think about the event and answer the questions "who," "what," "when," "where," and "why." Example:

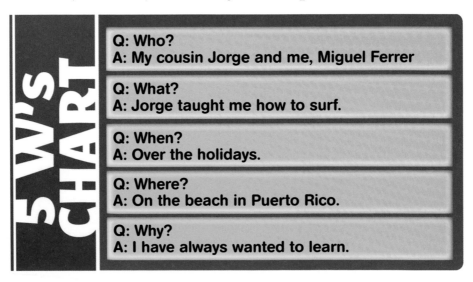

5 W'S CHART

Q: Who?
A: My cousin Jorge and me, Miguel Ferrer

Q: What?
A: Jorge taught me how to surf.

Q: When?
A: Over the holidays.

Q: Where?
A: On the beach in Puerto Rico.

Q: Why?
A: I have always wanted to learn.

By using this method, you can identify the important information you need to cover. Then, you can fill in the details of your experience.

FIRST-PERSON POINT OF VIEW

Personal writing pieces are often written using the first-person point of view. The story is told with pronouns such as "I," "me," and "mine." In addition, the piece often takes a subjective view. This means that the piece reveals the feelings, opinions, attitudes, and observations of the point-of-view character—in this case, the author. The subjective view enables the author to pour his or her heart and soul into the piece without holding back. The author can show exactly what was going through his or her mind during the event. Whether or not this creation will be read by anyone else, the point of the subjective view is to express the author's thoughts with freedom and honesty.

Going Deeper

After nailing down the basics, you can ask yourself more in-depth questions about the topic. Use a recording device or a pad of paper and pen and try "interviewing" yourself about the subject. Pretend you are a stranger wanting to know more about the experience. Imagine that this person is making a movie of your story. How would you describe the situation to him or her? How would the setting

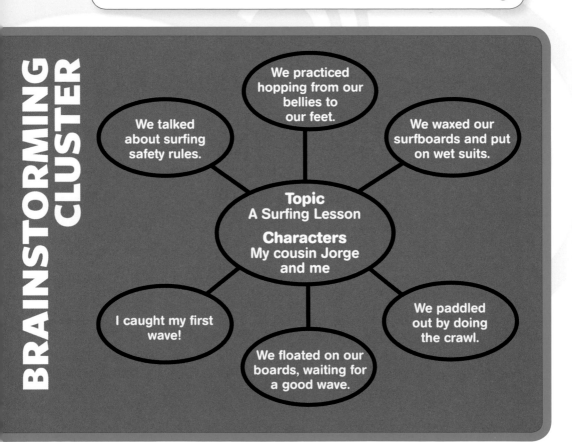

BRAINSTORMING CLUSTER

We practiced hopping from our bellies to our feet.

We talked about surfing safety rules.

We waxed our surfboards and put on wet suits.

Topic
A Surfing Lesson
Characters
My cousin Jorge and me

I caught my first wave!

We paddled out by doing the crawl.

We floated on our boards, waiting for a good wave.

appear? Write down all of the details. Another method is to create a brainstorming cluster, which you can use to write exact details about the event.

You can also find interesting information for your writing by searching the world around you. Your search may spark additional ideas. For example, books, music, and movies may remind you of details about your topic. If something pops into your head while you are reading, listening, or watching, write it down. Think about what music might have been playing during your experience, or how the event may remind you of a movie's or a book's story line.

These warm-up techniques will bring your topic into focus and give you a strong foundation on which to build. Before you begin drafting, make sure the subject you have chosen is tightly focused. This means that you are keeping the spotlight on just one moment in time,

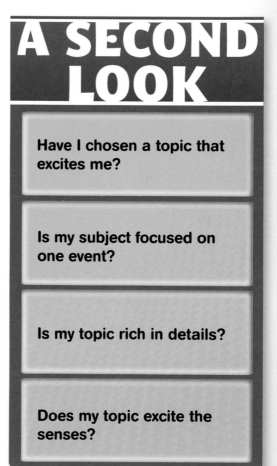

A SECOND LOOK

Have I chosen a topic that excites me?

Is my subject focused on one event?

Is my topic rich in details?

Does my topic excite the senses?

To add interesting details to your writing, look at a moment from a different perspective. For example, write about a moment from the viewpoint of a pet.

rather than bouncing from topic to topic.

Thinking Creatively

Considering a topic from a different viewpoint might help you notice details you have taken for granted. As a creative writing exercise, try taking your topic and writing about it from the viewpoint of someone (or something!) else.

For instance, how would your dog or cat see the situation, or your mom, or a celebrity? If you are writing about your birthday, consider writing about it from the point of view of another person at the party, such as your best friend, a late or unexpected guest, or an outsider looking in. You might even try writing from the viewpoint or perspective of an inanimate object, such as a piñata or a backpack. Play around with different variations and see if any spark your interest. You'll be surprised to learn how changing the point of view in any situation can alter the story's focus, drama, or creative expression.

chapter 3

Creating a First Draft

Personal writing can have a tone that is humorous or serious, depending on how it is presented. A piece can also be organized in different ways. In the process of creating a first draft, you will make decisions about your piece's tone and organization, giving it a sense of direction.

Teachers often tell students to write the way they speak. In the case of personal writing, this is especially true. As you write your draft, pretend that you are telling your story to a friend. This technique will help your unique writer's voice to shine through more easily.

Mixing It Up: Organizing Your Piece

No matter what writing style you choose, you'll need to pick an interesting

ESSENTIAL STEPS

Establish your author's voice and tone.

Decide how you will organize your story.

Write a first draft.

point from which to begin your story. As you start your draft, think about how you would like to introduce your subject. In many cases, the story can be told in chronological or time order, describing the situation from the beginning to the end. However, good writers sometimes rearrange the order of facts or other information in a story or poem to capture a reader's interest and heighten the drama.

There are many ways to organize a personal writing piece. One method is to begin in the middle of the action and then offer details about how you ended up in that situation. You can even begin the story at its end and explain the events in reverse. Here are some additional techniques to try:

- **Order of importance.** Instead of arranging information chronologically, try arranging the details of your narrative in the order of greatest importance.
- **Compare and contrast.** Explain the details of an event by comparing it to another one that is similar or to one that is very different.
- **Start at the climax.** Start your story by beginning with the most exciting details at the height of the action. Or, reverse this method and recall some subtle details first, working your way to an exciting finish.

FIGURATIVE LANGUAGE

With all good writing, it's important to use effective figurative language to describe an event. Listed below are some useful descriptive devices that can enhance any writing. However, be careful: figurative language should be added sparingly.

Hyperbole An exaggerated statement that stretches the truth. *The paintings on the wall were so bright that you needed sunglasses just to look at them.*

Personification Giving human characteristics to something that is not human. *The grilled cheese sandwich in the cafeteria cried out to be eaten.*

Simile To compare two different things using "like" or "as." *My grandmother's fuzzy sweater was as soft as a pillow.*

Metaphor To compare two different things without using "like" or "as." *My grandmother's fuzzy sweater was a soft pillow.*

One Story, Three Ways

The same event can be described using different writing forms and methods of organization. Think carefully about your topic and then decide which form is most suitable for engaging the reader.

As an example, the following narrative tells about the day the author's sister was born. The author chooses to start the story in the middle of the action:

Document1

They were behind the glass window, wiggling and crying. I'd never seen so many babies in one place! I was standing there because I'd gotten up to take a walk after my grandmother had asked me to stop making so much noise. I'd been nervously snapping a rubber watchband against my wrist for the last hour. I really didn't notice that I'd been doing it, but we were both impatiently waiting for my baby sister to be born. It seemed like we'd been waiting forever!

We had arrived at the hospital around two o'clock that morning and now it was 5 AM. We knew that everything was fine because a nurse had come and told us so, but we were still worried.

Page 1   Sec 1   1/1   At   0/0   ○REC ○TRK ○EXT ○OVR

However, the same story can be told differently. This personal letter describes the same event, starting at the end of the action:

Document1

2304 Happy Lane
Supersville, MD 01920
May 10, 2011

Dear Sarah,

We just returned home with my baby sister and she's a beauty! Her eyes are green and her hair is curly. Her name is Phoebe and everyone loves her, although she doesn't do much of anything yet. While I watch her sleep, it reminds me of all the other little babies I saw at the hospital the morning she was born.

My grandmother and I were there for what seemed like forever, waiting for my mom to give birth. I had been annoying my grandmother by nervously snapping a rubber watchband against my wrist. I decided to take a walk around the hallways, which were decorated with colorful paintings of flowers, when I ended up staring through the glass at all the sleepy newborns. It seemed so strange.

Finally, after I returned from my walk, a nurse told us that Phoebe had been born! Do you remember when your little brother was born? Write me back.

Sincerely,
Audrey

Page 1   Sec 1   1/1   At 1"   Ln 1   Col 1   0/0   OVR

Finally, the author communicates the same actions and feelings in the form of a poem. The story is told in chronological order:

A SECOND LOOK

Have I chosen an effective form for my story?

Have I decided how to organize the piece?

Is my writing descriptive?

Am I being true to my memories and personal viewpoint?

Waiting for Phoebe

The doors open wide
at two o'clock in the morning
as mom rolls into the hospital
ready to deliver my baby sister.
Grandma, Daddy, and I trail
along behind.
Big, loud, blue, orange, and
red flowers
jump off the wall
as my mom and dad disap-
pear into a room
just for new moms.
I put my head on Grandma's
fuzzy sweater
and dream of tiny babies.
Snap, snap, snap
I spring my rubber watch-
band
as if to hurry the time.
Many hours later,
there she is:
the one and only Phoebe.

Audrey Brown

Writing a Draft

Once you have decided how you'd like to begin your draft, you're ready to write. Find a place to concentrate and have your notes handy. Don't concern yourself with spelling or punctuation at this point. Let your ideas and writing flow freely. With personal writing, it is important to keep going until all of your ideas are incorporated into your draft. You will have a

Once you get your juices flowing, you'll enjoy recording all of your ideas in a first draft.

chance to make corrections and add details later.

Follow your train of thought until you've come to its end. Your writing may seem to have a life of its own. You'll remember details and moments that you may have forgotten about earlier. Write everything down because once you've started, you'll probably find that you don't want to stop until everything's been told. Follow the story to its natural conclusion, like any journey. Fasten your seatbelt and let go!

chapter 4

Revising and Editing

Revising means improving your work and looking at it with a fresh eye. In this stage of the process, search for places to make your story clearer, bolder, or livelier. Pretend that you've never seen the writing before and find places to add interesting details.

This is also a good time to make sure your writing flows smoothly. With any type of writing, a good way to check its flow is by reading it aloud to yourself or to others. If you are sharing your work with someone, make sure he or she understands that you are sharing a draft. Personal writing is very creative, so be sure that anyone who reads your work at this stage respects what you are trying to do.

During the revision stage, the priority is to make sure your piece works as a story.

ESSENTIAL STEPS

Polish details to bring your writing to life.

Examine and improve sentence structure and word choice.

Complete a spelling and grammar check.

Proofread your draft.

Ways to Stretch a Moment

Since personal writing focuses on individual experiences, it is not necessary to support your work with a large number of facts. But you do need to give your readers enough detail that they can relate to and envision your story.

Friends can give you ideas about places to slow down a moment and add more description.

Authors use a number of techniques to bring personal writing to life. The best authors can "stretch" a moment, or pull the maximum amount of detail from a real-life moment and communicate it to the reader. As you review your first draft, make notes about sections where more description and detail might improve your writing. Then try one of the following tools of the writer's craft.

Zoom In and Out

When someone films a movie, he or she looks through the camera lens and chooses whether to zoom in to the action or bring the camera angle out to view a larger scene. Often in a movie, you'll get both viewpoints: the close-up and the long shot. You can also use these techniques in your personal writing.

To practice, think of something you do every day, such as brushing your teeth, and write about it using both of these viewpoints. First, describe the moment from a very close view (maybe with a description of the toothbrush). Then zoom out to reveal a wider angle. To do this, you might describe who is holding the toothbrush and how he or she appears in the surroundings of the bathroom. Using words as your "camera," describe what you see.

When revising your piece, find a specific moment in the story where you can "zoom in" to expand its detail. You can linger there for some time to enhance the effect. Describe what you see, including the light and any other tiny details.

Use Suspense

Authors also add extra suspense to a story by drawing out an edgy or tense moment. Find a moment in your story in which an exciting event is taking place and then make it twice as long as it was in real life. Think about when you drop something made of glass and it seems as if it takes forever to hit the ground. Apply that same treatment to your story.

Document1

When I was eight, I was determined to see if Santa Claus was an actual person. On Christmas Eve, I pretended I was asleep in my bed, and then, when I thought everyone else was asleep, I went downstairs and sat down next to the Christmas tree. I decided to stay there for a while to see what would happen. The lights on the tree were twinkling brightly. I started staring at them.

Suddenly I felt like I was in a trance. I noticed that the star, which was made of gold foil, had a little angel on it. I thought I saw her wink at me. I continued looking and noticed that her hair was golden, just like the star, and that her tiny wings were made of gauze. Just when I thought she was about to speak, I heard a loud noise.

Page 1   Sec 1   1/1   At 1"   REC TRK EXT OVR

Add Thoughts and Feelings

What we say both inside our heads—whether memories or reactions to the moment—or out loud to others can also add more detail to a story.

These and other techniques can help any writer stretch a moment and add vivid details to a personal writing piece. Try them and see what happens.

When reading, see if you can pick out examples of these techniques in works by your favorite

Document1

The noise was coming from outside. I thought that it could be Santa coming through the door—or it could be a burglar. I was paralyzed, not knowing what to do. Footsteps came closer. I felt a little sweat run down my back as the sound of heavy shoes moved right outside the door. My heart was pounding so loudly that I was sure whoever was out there could hear me.

Suddenly, I didn't want to know if Santa was real or not. The doorknob rattled, first slowly, then quickly, and then it stopped. I couldn't tell if the door was opening or not because by then, I had squeezed my eyes shut. I thought I was going to faint.

Page 1   Ln 1   Col 1   0/0   REC TRK EXT OVR

authors. A teacher or librarian can guide you to additional examples. These are often called "mentor texts" because you can use them as models for your writing.

Revising Words and Sentences

Once you have revised the major ideas and details of your piece, it is time to examine and improve the style and sound of your writing. First, make sure your piece has a variety of sentence styles

As I sat huddled in fear, I felt sure that it was a horrible thing for someone to come through that door. It was not all right for a strange man, even if it was Santa Claus, to come into our house while we were sleeping! In a flash, the door opened. I cried out, "Who are you? Go away!" Then I saw that it was my dad.

He froze like a statue and said, "Reece, what are you doing?"

I suddenly felt as if my Christmas was ruined. How was I going to get out of this? I thought of all sorts of excuses, like I'd only come down for a glass of water, or I wanted to check to make sure all the lights were turned off.

But dad smiled. He told me that he'd gone outside to make sure that Santa would have a smooth landing on our lawn since it was covered with decorations. I don't know if I believed him, but I was relieved that it was Dad who had come through the door.

and lengths. Using vivid, strong words is also important.

Varying Sentence Styles

To make your piece sound more interesting, be sure to vary the structure of your sentences. For example, the piece should include both complex and compound sentences.

PROOFREADING SYMBOLS

If you give your piece to someone else to proof-read, he or she may correct it with proofreading marks. Here is a guide to let you know what some of those symbols mean.

- Insert something ∧
- Delete ℓ
- Insert a comma ⌃
- Apostrophe or single quotation mark ˅
- Double quotation marks ⸌⸍ ˮ
- Transpose elements (switch the order) ∿
- Insert a space #
- Close up this space ⊃
- Use a period here ⊙
- Begin new paragraph ¶
- No paragraph no¶

When you take a thought that cannot stand alone—known as a dependent clause—and add it to a complete sentence, the sentence is called a complex sentence. Example:

> **The shiny blue bike, which my parents had been hiding for two months, was the best gift I ever received.**

The sentence "The shiny blue bike was the best gift I ever received" is complete on its own. However, the dependent clause "which my parents had been hiding for two months" adds a detail that gives the reader valuable information.

Joining two complete sentences that have both a subject and a verb creates a compound sentence. A semicolon or a conjunction ("and," "or," "but," or in the following case, "so") is used to connect the two sentences into one. These examples show the two different ways to create a compound sentence:

> **There are cupcakes, brownies, and cookies piled high on the table; it would be hard for anyone to pass up dessert.**

> **There are cupcakes, brownies, and cookies piled high on the table, so it would be hard for anyone to pass up dessert.**

Varying sentence structure, as well as the length of sentences, will help give your writing more rhythm. Be sure to examine the individual sentences that make up your story, poem, or journal entry for places where improvements can be made.

Improving Word Choice

If you find that you've used the same words repeatedly, mark them and then use a thesaurus to find alternative words. A thesaurus is a book of words and their synonyms. Synonyms are different words that have the same, or almost the same, meaning. For example, some synonyms for the verb "laugh" are "chuckle," "snicker," "cackle," and "guffaw." In addition to making your writing sound less repetitive, using synonyms can make your writing more precise. Did the person in your story simply "giggle," or did he or she "howl"? Choosing just the right word can help the reader get a stronger image.

Editing for Conventions

Finally, you can begin to put the finishing touches on your piece. It is time to check the conventions of your writing—things like spelling, grammar, capitalization, and punctuation.

For all types of writing, it is important to check spelling. If you've written your piece on a computer, use the spell-check function. If your work is handwritten, examine the piece and circle any questionable words. Then look those words up in a dictionary.

To correct grammar, check that you have used the correct forms of verbs and that your subjects and verbs agree. Many word processing programs will help you check grammar as well as spelling. For example, your computer's program may underline words in color to warn you about possible grammar errors. Correct capitalization and punctuation is also something you'll want to review.

A Final Review

Before creating a final version of a piece, writers do a final review to be sure the piece is the best it can be. Proofreading usually involves reading your work several times. Be sure to read your writing out loud at least once so that you can hear where it might sound awkward. Read your work line by line, and examine each sentence carefully. Make notes about words or sentences that you want to delete or replace. Finally, examine your work for any remaining errors in spelling, grammar, punctuation, or capitalization.

Because personal writing is something that comes from your heart and individual experiences, it can be helpful to enlist people with more distance to help with proofreading. In the case of a letter, read it aloud to a friend or family member before creating a final copy. If you are writing a journal entry, you may not want to share your work with anyone. However, it's always a good idea to find someone willing to review a narrative or poem before writing its final version.

Whether you are writing a letter to a pen pal or a story for publication, a proofreading partner can help you improve your piece.

You can pair up with a partner to exchange pieces or read your work aloud to a group. Explain to your partner(s) that you want to share thoughts in a constructive way. Constructive criticism should be useful and thoughtful.

A good way to gather constructive criticism is to hand out a list of specific items for the audience to review. They can make notes on each point to share with you once the reading is over. The following are examples of helpful questions:

- What part of the writing stands out most? Why?
- What part of the piece leaves you wanting more?
- Was anything in the piece unclear?
- Which details did you enjoy?
- Where can the writer add more details to bring his or her piece to life?
- Are there any other specific elements to improve?

Listen carefully to the reviewers' answers and see if you can use any of their suggestions. Jot down anything you do not want to forget.

This process usually works as a two-way street. At times, you'll be the one listening to and responding to someone else's writing. It's

A SECOND LOOK

Are there enough details in my piece to bring it to life?

Do I convey the excitement and importance of my personal moment?

Have I used a variety of sentence types and descriptive words?

Is there a natural flow to my writing?

Have I edited for conventions?

important to know how to be an active listener when someone is presenting his or her writing. Here are a few tips to keep in mind:

- Look directly at the presenter.
- Notice how the speaker uses his or her voice and hands.
- Write down any words that are new to you or that are confusing.
- Note something specific that the presenter has done well.
- Ask the presenter questions about anything that is unclear.

When the presenter is ready to hear your feedback, be sure to include positive points as well as negative ones. Also, to be most constructive, offer specific ways the author could make his or her work better.

chapter 5

Publishing Your Personal Writing

N ow that your personal piece has been completely written, it's time to put your work into its final form and create a copy that you'll be proud to present. There are a variety of ways that personal writing can be published and shared, from sharing informally with family and friends to sending your work out to magazines and writing contests.

Creating a Final Copy

First, make sure your name is displayed on the piece. It's important that you, the author, get credit for your work. If you've written a personal narrative or a poem, think about a title that would best reflect its content. Your title should

ESSENTIAL STEPS

Add final touches to your piece, such as a title.

Think about forums where you would like to share your work.

Create an attractive final copy appropriate for that setting.

contain enough information that potential readers will be curious about the piece and will want to read it. Titles are not necessary for letters or journal entries.

If your piece is a personal narrative, transfer your writing onto clean white paper using blue or black ink. If you are typing the piece on a computer, use a clear, easy-to-read font style and size. If a picture would add detail to your story, include one in a way that will not distract the reader.

If you are rewriting a poem, you can make its presentation fancier by using colored paper. You can also use more freedom in font style, size, and color when presenting poetry. If you are trying to convey a specific message with your poem, think about an appropriate way to present it. For instance, if you've written about a star, use a stencil to trace a star and write the poem inside it.

For letter writing, paper and font style are also important. Maybe the person to whom you are writing has a favorite color that can be used for paper or ink. You can also find or create pictures to add to the story. If you are describing a vacation, you could include a souvenir inside the letter, such as a leaf or a photograph.

In the case of journal writing, it's always nice to have a special book to record your thoughts. Find a blank book that appeals to you at a stationery shop,

START A CHAIN STORY

Creating a chain story can be a fun way to write by collaborating with others. Collaborative writing means that you have many writers working on one piece. One way to get this project in motion is to think about a memory and write a narrative paragraph about it. Send that paragraph to a friend. Ask your friend to add his or her own memory having to do with the same subject and then send it on to one of his or her friends to continue the chain. Do this until you have at least ten contributors.

Decide on the number of participants (such as ten) that you want to include at the beginning. Create a checklist for writers to mark off their name and number in the order. When the last person has checked off number ten, have him or her return the document to you. When you receive it, you can make copies for all the writers or send each a copy via e-mail. What you receive will contain ten different perspectives on one cool topic!

or go to an art supply store and buy one with a plain cover that you can personalize yourself.

Sharing Your Writing

Personal writing can be shared in a variety of ways. These range from putting together anthologies, which are collections of writings, to holding readings for friends and family. If you want to send your work into the professional writing world, you can ask an adult to help you search the Internet for magazines, newspapers, or Web sites that publish youth work. For example, the magazine *Stone Soup* publishes writing by young people. It also has a Web site (http://www.stonesoup.com) that offers students opportunities to submit their writing. Scholastic, Inc. also has a Web site (http://www.scholastic.com) where you and your teacher can share student writing and get feedback from

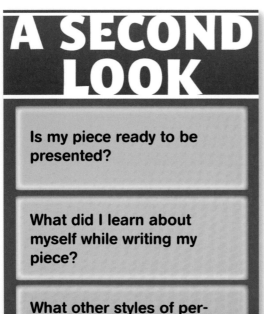

A SECOND LOOK

Is my piece ready to be presented?

What did I learn about myself while writing my piece?

What other styles of personal writing would I like to try?

professional and student authors.

Check out some additional options in the "Publishing and Posting" section of this book. If you decide to send your work to any of these places, follow their submission rules closely. Following submission guidelines carefully can help any writer make it past the rejection pile.

A more immediate way to gather feedback is to hold a reading with other writers and invite

Some teens find it rewarding to submit their best work to magazines or contests for possible publication.

people to listen to your work. To get inspiration, you can attend author readings at local bookstores or libraries. Check the newspaper or online listings to see if any businesses or organizations in your area hold such events. Going to public readings is a great way to see how authors present their works.

chapter 6

Personal Writing in the Digital Age

On the Internet, you can find a real audience for your personal writing all over the world. Are you interested in exchanging stories with young people in other schools and towns? Would you like to have readers as far away as South Africa or New Zealand? You can.

Publishing your work online allows you to get quick feedback from a wide variety of people and share thoughts and ideas with others. By using digital tools, you can join a worldwide community of writers.

Digital tools allow you to be especially creative in sharing your personal stories. In addition to publishing text, you can enhance your stories with digital art, photography, video, and audio.

ESSENTIAL STEPS

Set up your own blog, or start posting on a classroom blog.

Choose a few specific topics or genres to blog about regularly.

Join the community of bloggers by commenting on others' posts.

Blog About It

One of the most exciting ways to share your personal writing is by blogging. A blog (short for Weblog) is a digital journal that can serve many different purposes.

Writing a blog is similar to writing a journal or diary, except that the entries are posted online for the public to see. The entries, called blog posts, appear in reverse chronological order. The newest post appears on the top of the page, and the earlier posts appear below it. If you have enough old posts, you can store them in files called archives, where visitors can still access them.

Some blogs are like personal journals. For example, you can use a blog to write regularly about what is going on in your life. Each new post covers the latest news in your personal world. Other blogs are used to share interesting news about a particular topic, such as hip-hop music, vegetarian cooking, or baseball. Many classrooms have blogs in which teachers and students describe what they have been working on and learning. Blogs are also used to publish creative writing, such as poetry, stories, and humor.

Blogs are different from paper journals because you can enhance your personal writing with multiple

Blogging is a way to share your thoughts and ideas with a larger audience on the Internet.

forms of media. For example, you can record a podcast of a poem or story in your own voice and include it in your post. Then readers can hear your writing with the rhythm, tone of voice, and emotion that you intended. You can choose music to play in the background as well. To add a visual element, you can include computer-designed or scanned artwork, photos, or video clips to go along with your writing. Using digital tools, you can tell personal stories through a media collage.

A Two-Way Street

Like other forms of personal writing, blogging is a great way to develop your author's voice and share your unique perspective on any topic. However, blogging is more interactive than paper publishing.

Readers of blogs can leave comments, so any post can become a discussion with others. From others' feedback on your work, you can learn what worked well and what did not. Readers' comments may also spark new ideas.

BLOGS, BLOGS, EVERYWHERE

Blogs are an exciting tool because they allow anyone to publish their writing. While adult professionals write many blogs, discussing topics such as politics and entertainment, young people with ideas can write blogs, too. Using services such as Blogger, WordPress, and LiveJournal, individuals can set up blogs easily and for free. Through services like Edublogs, many teachers set up blogs that their classes can work on as a group. As a result, millions of adults and young people maintain blogs as a hobby. The Web site BlogPulse (http://www.blogpulse.com) reports that there are at least 150 million blogs on the Web, and the number grows daily.

Blogs allow people to develop relationships with others, forming a community of readers and writers. People with similar interests may start to follow your blog, reading it on a regular basis. They may have their own blogs as well, so you can read and comment on their posts in return. Many bloggers link to each others' sites through a list of favorite blogs called a blogroll. They also link to other Web sites they think their readers will enjoy or find helpful. Best of all, bloggers encourage, inspire, and motivate each other to keep creating more work on their blogs.

Blog Netiquette

Netiquette, which means Web etiquette, is guidelines that help everyone have a positive experience online. When you become a blogger and a reader of other blogs, it is important to add to the conversation in a positive and constructive way. There are a number of do's and don'ts to follow when interacting with others on blogs. First, here are some of the do's:

- Make comments that are related to the content of the post. Continue the dialogue started by the blogger or by other readers.
- Acknowledge the author. Let the blogger know what you liked about his or her

writing, or what it made you think about. Thank the blogger if you learned something from a post.

- Provide something that adds to the discussion, such as a Web link or new idea. Share your experiences and unique perspective.
- Let the author know if you agree with him or her. Explain why or why not. Back up your statements with examples or evidence.
- You can challenge someone's point of view, but always do so respectfully.

Certain behaviors are important to avoid in the blogosphere, or the world of blogs. Here are some important don'ts:

- Never attack anyone personally or call anyone names.
- Do not use bad language or words that will offend others.
- Do not write comments in all capital letters. It is considered shouting.

A SECOND LOOK

Are my blog posts interesting and thought provoking?

Have I included Web links and multimedia elements in my posts?

Am I making thoughtful comments on other people's blogs?

- Do not share your or other people's last names, addresses, phone numbers, personal photos, physical locations, or other personal information. This is not safe.
- Do not respond to someone who asks you for personal information or who makes you uncomfortable in any way. Tell a parent or teacher.

Overall, remember that the Web is a public forum. Unless you set up a blog that can only be read with a password or by friends in a network, most blogs are not private. Everyone, from your neighbors to your grandparents, can view the material that is posted. Make sure you are proud of any work you post and that any comments you write are appropriate.

We have discussed many different types of personal writing in this book, and hopefully, there are plenty of ideas that sound appealing. Personal writing can be a way to communicate with distant family and friends, a way of rethinking your thoughts and ideas, or a therapeutic method of sorting out your day. Whatever the reason for beginning your creative journey, speak your mind and express yourself!

GLOSSARY

author's voice The distinct style and personality that every writer brings to his or her work.

blog A blog is a Web page that serves as an online journal for an individual.

blogger A person who writes a blog.

chronological Arranged in the order of time.

description A form of writing that allows the reader to see, smell, hear, taste, and feel what the author has written about; a picture in words.

feedback The return of information evaluating one's work.

figurative language A phrase that departs from a literal meaning in order to compare items or get an image across.

journal A daily written record of personal experiences and observations.

memoir An account of the writer's life and experiences.

meter A rhythmic pattern of stressed and unstressed syllables in poetry.

personal narrative Writing that tells a true story about an event or series of events in the author's life.

podcast A digital audio file similar to a radio broadcast.

subjective view The point of view in which the reader knows the thoughts and feelings of one character.

submission A writing entry to be considered for publication.

tone The author's attitude or mood, which may be formal, informal, friendly, angry, etc.

FOR MORE INFORMATION

826 National

826 Valencia Street

San Francisco, CA 94110

(415) 642-5905 Ext. 204

Web site: http://www.826national.org

826 National is a nonprofit tutoring, writing, and publishing organization with locations in eight U.S. cities.

Alliance for Young Artists & Writers

557 Broadway

New York, NY 10012

(212) 343-6493

Web site: http://www.artandwriting.org

This nonprofit organization identifies teens in grades 7–12 with excep-
tional artistic and literary talent and brings their work to a national
audience through the Scholastic Art & Writing Awards.

Girls Write Now, Inc.

247 West 37th Street, Suite 1800

New York, NY 10018

(212) 336-9330

Web site: http://www.girlswritenow.org/gwn

Girls Write Now provides youth mentoring and rigorous creative-writ-
ing instruction within the context of fun, all-girl programming.

League of Canadian Poets

312-192 Spadina Avenue

Toronto, ON M5T 2C2

Canada

(416) 504-1657

Web sites: http://www.poets.ca

http://www.youngpoets.ca

This nonprofit arts organization works to promote poetry in Canada and to promote Canadian poetry around the world.

Publishing and Posting

Below is a list of publications and Web sites that welcome submissions from young writers.

Merlyn's Pen

11 South Angell Street, Suite 301

Providence, RI 02906

(401) 751-3766

E-mail: merlyn@merlynspen.org

Web site: http://www.merlynspen.org

New Moon Girls

P.O. Box 161287

Duluth, MN 55816

(800) 381-4743

E-mail: help@newmoon.com

Web site: http://www.newmoon.com

Skipping Stones

P.O. Box 3939

Eugene, OR 97403

(541) 342-4956

E-mail: info@skippingstones.org

Web site: http://www.skippingstones.org

Web Sites

Due to the changing nature of Internet links, Rosen Publishing has developed an online list of Web sites related to the subject of this book. This site is updated regularly. Please use this link to access the list:

http://www.rosenlinks.com/wlp/wps

FOR FURTHER READING

Codell, Esmé Raji. *Sing a Song of Tuna Fish: A Memoir of My Fifth-Grade Year*. New York, NY: Hyperion Paperbacks for Children, 2006.

Fletcher, Ralph J. *How to Write Your Life Story*. New York, NY: Scholastic, 2010.

Fletcher, Ralph J. *Marshfield Dreams: When I Was a Kid*. New York, NY: Henry Holt & Co., 2005.

Friot, Bernard. *The Aspiring Poet's Journal*. New York, NY: Abrams Books for Young Readers, 2008.

Mack, James. *Journals and Blogging* (Culture in Action). Chicago, IL: Raintree, 2009.

INDEX

ABOUT THE AUTHORS

Jaye E. Cook is a writer and educator in New York City.

Lauren Spencer has taught writing workshops in New York City public schools. She also writes culture and lifestyle articles for magazines.

PHOTO CREDITS

Cover, pp. 21, 26, 35 Shutterstock.com; pp. 4–5 John Howard/ Lifesize/Thinkstock; p. 8 Gabriela Maj/Getty Images; p. 33 Jupiterimages/Creatas/Thinkstock; p. 44 Comstock/Thinkstock; pp. 51, 54 Fuse/Getty Images.

Editor: Andrea Sclarow; Photo Researcher: Karen Huang